CARL PHILIPP EMANUEL BACH

CONCERTO

IN D MINOR

FOR

PIANO

AND

ORCHESTRA

Wq23 - H427

3091

SUGGESTIONS FOR USING THIS MMO EDITION

WE HAVE TRIED to create a product that will provide you an easy way to learn and perform a concerto with a full orchestra in the comfort of your own home. Because it involves a fixed orchestral performance, there is an inherent lack of flexibility in tempo and cadenza length. The following MMO features and techniques will reduce these inflexibilities and help you maximize the effectiveness of the MMO practice and performance system:

Where the soloist begins a movement *solo*, we have provided an introductory measure with subtle taps inserted at the actual tempo before the soloist's entrance.

Chapter stops on your CD are conveniently located throughout the piece at the beginnings of practice sections, and are cross-referenced in the score. This should help you quickly find a desired place in the music as you learn the piece.

Chapter stops have also been placed at orchestra entrances (after cadenzas, for example) so that, with the help of a second person, it is possible to perform a seamless version of the concerto alongside your MMO CD accompaniment. While we have allotted what is generally considered an average amount of time for a cadenza, each performer will have a different interpretation and observe individ-

ual tempi. Your personal rendition may preclude a perfect "fit" within the space provided. Therefore, by having a second person press the pause ❚❚ button on your CD player after the start of each cadenza, followed by the next track ▶▶❙ button, your CD will be cued to the orchestra's re-entry. When you as soloist are at the end of the cadenza or other solo passage, the second person can press the play ▶ (or pause ❚❚ button) on the CD remote to allow a synchronized orchestra re-entry.

Regarding tempi: again, we have observed generally accepted tempi, but some may wish to perform at a different tempo, or to slow down or speed up the accompaniment for practice purposes. You can purchase from MMO (or from other audio and electronics dealers) specialized CD players which allow variable speed while maintaining proper pitch. This is an indispensable tool for the serious musician and you may wish to look into purchasing this useful piece of equipment for full enjoyment of all your MMO editions.

We want to provide you with the most useful practice and performance accompaniments possible. If you have any suggestions for improving the MMO system, please feel free to contact us. You can reach us by e-mail at mmogroup@musicminusone.om.

Music Minus One

3091

CARL PHILIPP
EMANUEL
BACH

CONCERTO

IN D MINOR
FOR PIANO AND ORCHESTRA
WQ23 - H427

MMO 3091

CARL PHILIPP EMANUEL BACH: A SON FOR THE AGES

CARL PHILIPP EMANUEL BACH was born in Weimar on 8 March 1714 and died seventy-four years later in Hamburg on 14 December 1788. He is without question the most famous and prolific son of Johann Sebastian Bach. Known during his lifetime for his brilliant keyboard artistry, he was and still is immensely respected for his compositions and for his work as a theorist.

Emanuel (the name he was known by) was the second son of J. S. Bach by his first wife Maria Barbara, and descended on both sides of his family from musicians. One of his godfathers was none other than Georg Phillip Telemann, who, despite the elder Bach's reputation, was considered the most esteemed composer of his generation (a position J. S. Bach has since usurped). With a father and godfather such as these two men, young Emanuel had much to live up to. As his life story relates, he did just that.

In his short autobiography, Emanuel states that he never had any other musical training than that he received from his father, nor on any other instrument than the keyboard. It was presumably due to this intense concentration, under the scrutiny and direction of so remarkable a father, that Emanuel could reputedly sight-read his father's keyboard pieces by the age of eleven. Clearly here was a musically gifted child who was both born into the right family and who received an education conducive to his musical development.

His musical instincts were astounding. With the help of his father's own Olympian musical brilliance, Emanuel came to be exposed to a world of music unlike any other child (aside from his own siblings, of course). In his earliest consciousness, the boy was exposed to the rich world of French and Italian music that his father loved so much. Possibly even more influential were the constant flow of visitors Emanuel came to meet in the hospitable Bach home in Cothen, outside of Leipzig. These weren't just ordinary visitors, this was the *crème* of European musical culture, and the young Emanuel relished their performances. There can be little question that, musically, the Bach household was the richest of its day.

Beyond the musical training he received from his father, Emanuel got a fine education at Thomasschule, where his father oversaw the subject of music. He logically moved on to the nearby University of Leipzig in 1731, all the while living at home and assuming the rôle of his father's principal assistant.

What is surprising is that Emanuel matriculated at Leipzig in law, not music. He moved on to the University of Frankfurt an der Oder, where he was accepted in 1734 and remained until 1738. We can only hypothesize the reasons for this odd maneuver—such as his taking for granted his own musical gifts; or a rebellious break with a family tradition that came from both his mother and father; or the longing to experience more of life than that of the musical world which had dominated his life and the lives of everyone around him. But these are only matters of conjecture, and are still debated endlessly by scholars.

The most probable reason is also the dullest. Quite simply, Emanuel's father encouraged his son to study law, as he also did with two of his other sons. Sebastian Bach, without a university education himself, never wanted his sons to suffer the indignities from court and church bureaucrats that he was forced to endure as a musician throughout his career. As the Bach family knew only too well, musicians of that period were often considered both ignorant and ordinary. Emanuel seemed to be especially sensitive to this injustice, since during his long life, there is no doubt that he could hold his own with anyone—intellectually, legally, and musically.

By the age of twenty-four, Carl Phillip Emanuel Bach had lived for several years in the musically deprived town of Frankfurt an der Oder, where he supported himself mostly by giving keyboard lessons and by composing for minor civic and church events while he was studying law. But it was at this point that Emanuel made the biggest decision in his life—he chose a career in music. The position which was ultimately offered him certainly had its ego-gratifications, for it was to be none other than that of harpsichordist to the court of Frederick the Great of Prussia, in Potsdam, just outside of Berlin. Emanuel took the job with alacrity and held it for thirty years, during which time he became known as the most famous keyboard player and teacher in Europe.

Having such a stable position at court enabled Emanuel to spend much time composing, and as Frederick's considerable power and influence grew across Europe, this helped, in turn, to promote his court musicians. Frederick was a noted amateur flutist and composer for that instrument; and the most important musician at court was Quantz, who was both Frederick's former flute teacher and the principle court flutist (after the king himself). Frederick had an immense love of music in general—he was a talented composer— and made his court the most musically conscious of its day.

The flute reigned at the Potsdam court just as powerfully as did Frederick; the vast majority of concerts heard were for that instrument. This frustrated Emanuel, but allowed him a great deal of time for teaching, composing and theorizing. Although Frederick's musical tastes were highly conservative, he helped turn Berlin into a center of enlightened thought. This was an appropriate environment for the independently minded

Emanuel; in 1753 he published the first of his considerable musical theories in *Versuch über die wahre Art des Clavier zu spielen (Essay on the True of Playing Keyboard Instruments)*. Widely influential, this work established Emanuel as the leading keyboard artist of the day.

Emanuel became increasingly dissatisfied with Frederick, particularly after he refused to compensate his court musicians for their losses during the Seven Years' War in 1756-1763 (during which time no music was allowed at court). He sought employment elsewhere. Against Frederick's will, he next took on the position of Kantor and music director in Hamburg, which had been the advantageous former position of his godfather, Telemann.

Although this was an enormously busy job, Hamburg's environment of free enterprise was much more to Emanuel's tastes. His influence and importance widened yet further, and he found many opportunities to display his long-suppressed entrepreneurial talents. He composed much church music in these later years, expanding his range yet further, adding to an already mountainous catalogue of compositions.

By the time of his death in 1788, Carl Philipp Emanuel Bach had achieved, not unlike his father, a body of achievements far beyond the scope of several men, let alone one person. He single-handedly promoted the *Empfindsamer* style characterized by severe contrasts in dynamics to introduce a highly charged feeling of emotion into keyboard music, an idea which—though maximally expressed on the clavichord, an instrument which would not survive the 18th century—would have profound repercussions for the developing pianoforte. His genius and contributions were lauded by Haydn, by Mozart and by Beethoven, and his advancement of the keyboard arts cannot be overestimated.

—*Douglas Scharmann*

C. Ph. E. Bach's Concerto in D Minor, Wq23/H427

Carl Philip Emanuel Bach's music for keyboard (clavichord, harpsichord, early piano, organ) follows a general artistic line in his entire compositional activities. Achievements from the Berlin period (1741-1768) are the Prussian sonatas for piano (devoted to King Friedrich II) from 1742/1743, and later the Würtenberg sonatas from 1744. In this period—the 1740s and the beginning of the 1750s—C. Ph. E. Bach was a major participant in the chamber music evenings at the royal court of Frederick the Great, accompanying the flute concerti of Johann Quantz, as well as his own concerti for flute and orchestra with Friedrich II as soloist.

From 1741 to the beginning of the Seven Years' War (1756-1763)—each year the composer wrote either one concerto or a series of concerti for piano and orchestra—around twenty-seven in all. These comprise the greater part of his more than fifty concerti for piano and orchestra. Among them is the present concerto for piano and string orchestra—D minor, Wq (Alfred Wottquenne) 23; H (Eugene Helm) 427, written in 1748. Just before this concerto, in 1747, Bach composed his popular concerto for flute and string orchestra in the same key, which is the original version of the last of the four concerti for piano and orchestra—the concerto in D minor, Wq22; H 425. In this manner all of his ten concerti for other instruments—flute, oboe, violoncello—are alternate versions of his piano concerti.

At approximately this time came the visit of Johann Sebastian Bach to the court of Frederick the Great, which is one of the most considerable events both in Berlin's musical history as well as in the biography of the father and son Bach. This visit became a cause for the writing of such compositions as "Musikalisches Opfer," and was most likely an impulse for the creative activity of C. Ph. E. Bach. Proof of this is the spacious, brilliant concerto for piano and orchestra in D minor, Wq23. A relatively short time after this came the creation of another of the composer's famous piano concerti—the one in A minor (1750), Wq26, with alternate versions for flute and orchestra and for violoncello and orchestra.

The piano concerti of C. Ph. E. Bach, as well as those of Johann Christian Bach, take an important place between their father's keyboard concerti and those of Wolfgang Amadeus Mozart. Unsurprisingly, the concerti of C. Ph. E. Bach are in the typical Bach-Vivaldi layout of the three movements—fast, slow, fast—but with the slow movement playing an increasing rôle as a center for musical development. They show a good balance between soloist and orchestra, in which each has an auspicious opportunity to uphold his sound abilities in front of a large audience, at big concert halls. This leads to a more spacious piano exposition when comparing it to the one in the solo piano pieces. In these as well as in the composer's other piano works (sonatas, rondos, fantasies, miniatures, variations) shines the piano virtuosity of the younger Bach, one that combines the best traditions of the 18th century—not only his so-called *Empfindsamer* style, but also from the brilliant idiom of the harpsichord performance styles of Domenico Scarlatti, and also of his piety for the rich melismatics of the French school. C. Ph. E. Bach's preference for the clavichord for the interpretation of his most private emotional expression is confronted with the fact that the clavichord never became popular outside of Germany. Right after 1740, he played on an early piano—the "Silbermann" Hammerflügel in the Charlottenburg Palace. He composed increasingly for the newly popular klavier—the piano—in the last two decades of his life.

A gradual evolution in the piano style of C. Ph. E. Bach is reflected in his piano parts (especially in his piano concerti). Unlike the contrapuntal exposition so prevalent in the musical language of J. S. Bach, there is a slight differentiation in the parts of each of the two hands in the texture, with a dominance in the solo rôle of the right hand. The melodic line, as well as the diverse harmonic figurations, are concentrated in the right hand's part. The rôle of these figurations in the binding and developing parts of the form is increasing. The part of the left hand is significantly differentiated and plays a simple function of accompanying the other hand. A typical kind of accompaniment is the repetition of single tones, harmonic intervals in the bass line. The drumming basses—the repetition of one tone in the bass—underlines the active character of the musical events in the fast parts of the concerti.

Most interesting are the unexpected bold *subito* harmonic moves, underlined with dramatic *timbre*-dynamic contrasts with impressive tonal modulations as well, accomplished with richly unfolded passages, in which the movement is divided between the two hands. Daring jumps through the whole range of the instrument are often combined with other elements of the piano technique—ornaments and scale-like passages, as well as with rushes in the expanded upper register (c^3-f^3) of the early piano. In the slow parts the abundance of various and complex rhythmical figures, which creates the impression of written *rubato*, is combined with the expressive manner of performing and reaching to the *cantilena* of the piano in the building of the poetical *Adagio* and *Andante*. In this building process a sense of piano improvisation is created.

This is why Josef Haydn wrote that he was greatly indebted to the piano works of C. Ph. E. Bach, and W. A. Mozart saw him as the father of the musicians of his time. This good opinion by his contemporaries is also due to C. Ph. E. Bach's prominent pedagogical work—*Versuch über die wahre Art, des Clavier zu spielen*. This work, together with the works of J. Quantz and Leopold Mozart, became a basic methodical reference on questions of musical performance. With it he became the precursor of the piano virtuosity so prevalent in the 19th century. C. Heefe taught Beethoven by this work and that master later taught his own students in Vienna according to it. The work should not be reviewed as a summary of the personal experience of a great musician. Rather it is a summary of the rich piano-performing theory and practice in the 18th century. Bach rests not only on the traditions of the German piano art, but also synthesizes the best achievements of the differing national schools. This is the direction in which the new classical style of the Vienna school was founded.

As a composer C. Ph. E. Bach combines his preference for piano improvisation with the strictness of the form, usually resting on one theme and its free transformation. The closeness between the three main thematic lines in the solo piano part in the D-minor Concerto for Piano and Orchestra (1748) Wq 23—is underlined.

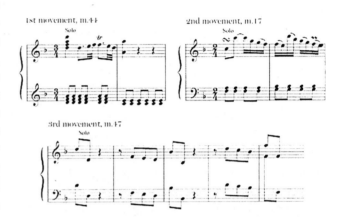

In the exposition of these thematic lines, as well as in the whole unfolding in the musical development, particularly in part 3, appears the strength and the universal appeal of a style leading to Beethoven.

In the first part of the concerto there are long spaces, with an approach towards a wide harmonic rhythm and the regular phraseology of the classical style. Against the background of repeated tones, in a dialogue between the soloist and the high strings, a panting melody unfolds, with a wide scale—first and second octave. The dramatic expression and tense mode of the first theme changes with the hesitant, short phrases of the second theme, which are perceived as exclamations and sighs in the emotional speech. Also, the second theme in G minor unfolds through a dialogue-like form; A^7 harmony incites to the figuration of a virtuoso piano solo that later transits into an *ad libitum* cadenza, and after a second *fermata* on a trill on the 6th degree, pours an expressive cadenza written by the composer, the end of which is dashingly accented by the orchestral introduction to the preliminary stage of the first movement's development section. The dialogue between soloist and orchestra is enriched with new harmonic combinations, in which different elements of the theme are combined.

The tension is maintained by the skillful orchestration (alternations of the "anxious" short trills in the strings—at one moment in the violins, at another in the violas or in the basses—violoncello and contrabass), by the changing the direction of the developmental solo rushes of the piano, by the broken rhythms and the rapid alternation one after another of dynamic contrasts (m. 179-194). It is also kept by the piano cadenza in A minor that prepares and leads to a false orchestral *reprise* in the same tonality. Again a piano expression (m. 221-252) with richly unfolded 16th-note figurations on the scales of the harmonic intervals—triads and D7—in the right-hand part pushes smoothly but surely towards the true *reprise*: one that sounds with the original strength and expression (m. 253), but is now enriched with the new shades brought by the harmonic passages towards the second theme, which sounds in the original tonality—D minor. Again a cadenza, like the first one (before the development), but now leading to D minor, outlines in *pomposo* manner the final intonations, and shoulders the form of the entire *Allegro* movement.

The slow movements in the piano concerti of C. Ph. E. Bach are touching, elegiac poems. In a carefully crafted sound picture (*Poco Andante* in the concerto in D minor) the orchestra creates a rich atmosphere ornamented with various and unusually melismatic piano solos. The orchestral introductions (like Beethoven's Piano Concerto No. 4 in G major) become more and more insistent and the piano's comments are exquisite and compassionate in their nature, extracting thrilling sounds of sorrow and hope, of compassion and exclamation. The final cadenza leads to the push of the chained syncopations in the violins and a united rhythmic orchestral conclusion.

The third movement—*Allegro assai*—impresses with its short, objective, "Beethoven-like" phrases, filled with boiling energy, with the sharp changes in *timbre* and dynamics, as well as with the voluminous, spacious expositions of orchestra and soloist. Once again there are rapid changes in the piano part (m. 64-114). Alternations of bright thematic images and of the expressive elements build, and the orchestra is left in an intense development of the original thematic sphere. This builds a *rondo*-variation form, distinguished by wide "terraced" spaces, in which the sequential intermediates unfold.

A false *reprise* (again as in the first part) originally in the orchestra (m. 278), and later in the piano part, enriches the development of the third movement and outlines the whole form of the concerto. Against the backdrop of "hidden" tension in the legato notes carried across the barline verticals (m. 386-418) the "running" sixteenth figurations in the piano part lead logically to the final thematic implementation. This is followed by an extravagant *fugato* between pianist and strings and—even more expressively—in its unexpectedly monodic solo in the composer's own cadenza. But they outline the density and the shining qualities of the unison movements in the orchestral conclusion in *forte*.

So ends a concerto in which not only is it C. Ph. E. Bach's personal ambition to unfold a massive form, but in which his ability to achieve an interesting musical development is also in evidence. It remains a remarkable example of the early piano style fomenting at the approach of the second half of the 18th century, and it holds a valuable place in the evolution of the genre of the piano concerto.

—*Romeo Smilkov*

A NOTE ON THE EDITION

In creating this authoritative performance edition, the editor consulted the following sources:
- the autograph manuscript kept in Berlin;
- the critical edition published in Volumes 29-30 of the *Denkmäler deutscher Tonkunst*, 1906;
- the edition of Gabor Darvas, Editio Musica Budapest, 1968;
- the edition of Gertrud Wertheim, Breitkopf & Härtel (Wiesbaden), 1956

Performance Notes to
Carl Philipp Emanuel Bach's Piano works
(from the foreword by Carl Krebs in his 1895 edition)

Bemerkungen zu
Carl Philipp Emanuel Bach Klavierwerken
(Aus dem Vorwort von Carl Krebs zur Ausgabe von 1895)

Die Vorschlage :
Lange Vorsschläge

Die Triller
"Er nimt allzeit seinen Anfafg von der Secunde über den Ton ..." *

Der Triller von unten

Der Triller von oben

Der halbe oder Pralltriller

Der Mordent a) lang

b) kurz

Die Doppelschläge

Der prallende Doppelschlag

Der geschnellte Doppelschlag

Der Doppelschlag von unten

Der Schneller

Der Anschlag

Doppelgrifen

Der Schleifer
von zwei Noten   von drei Noten

*) Carl Philipp Emanuel Bach "Versuch über die wahre Art, das Clavier zu spielen"

Concerto in D minor

for Piano and Strings†
(Potsdam, 1748)

Edited with orchestral reduction
by Romeo Smilkov

CarlPhilipp Emanuel Bach
Wq23; H427

†The full original title of the work reads: "Concerto per il Cembalo concerto, accompagnato da due Violini,
Violetta e Basso".

*) The dynamics and tempo markings in brackets, as well as the additional musical text in the solo part engraved
with small notes, are suggestions from the editor.

Vorschlag zur Verzierung der Fermate:

CADENZA (C.Ph.E.Bach)

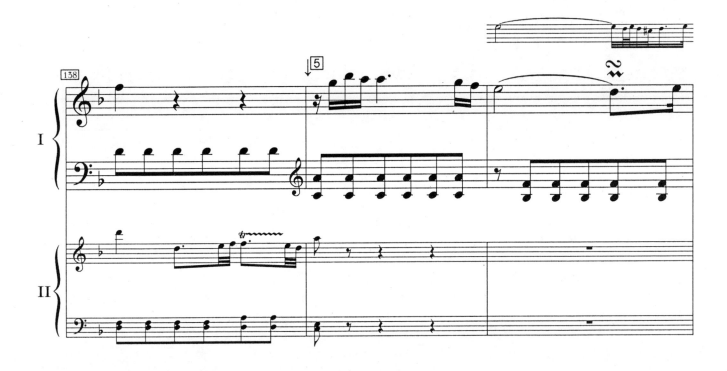

22

32

MMO 3091

34

Vorschlag zur Verzierung der Fermate:

ad lib.

CADENZA (C.Ph.E.Bach)

MMO 3091

II.

Poco Andante (♩=72)

Vorschlag zur Verzierung der Fermate (Gertrud Wertheim):

CADENZA
(C.Ph.E.Bach)

III.

48

MMO 3091

50

56

58

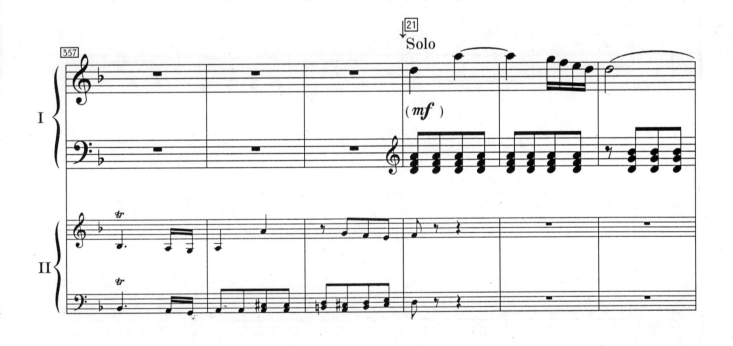

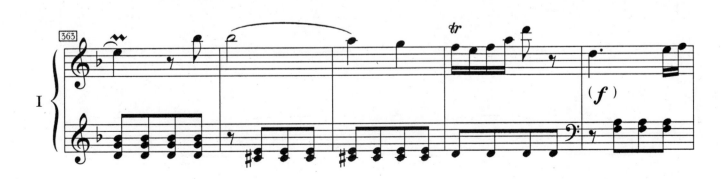

68

CADENZA (C.Ph.E.Bach)

*)Vorschlag zur Verzierung der Fermate (Gertrud Wertheim):

CADENZA

Engraving: Wieslaw Nowak

MMO 3091

MUSIC MINUS ONE
50 Executive Boulevard
Elmsford, New York 10523-1325
800-669-7464 (U.S.)/914-592-1188 (International)

www.musicminusone.com
e-mail: mmogroup@musicminusone.com

MUSIC MINUS ONE

Vocal
Catalogue

Opera with Orchestra

MMO is proud to present the finest arias in the operatic repertoire now available, with full orchestral accompaniment! We have brought the finest European vocalists and orchestras together to create an unparalleled experience–giving you the opportunity to sing opera the way it was meant to be performed. All titles are now CD+Graphics encoded so that you can see the lyrics on your television screen in real-time–and, as always, the full printed vocal score is included as well.

SOPRANO

Soprano Arias · MMO CDG 4052
Zvetelina Maldjanska–Vidin Philharmonic/Todorov

Puccini La Bohème – *Mi chiamano Mimi (Mimi)*; **Mozart** Die Zauberflöte – *Ach, ich fühl's*; **Verdi** I Vespri Siciliani – *Siciliana d'Elena*; **Bizet** Les Pecheurs de Perles – *Me voilà seule dans la nuit*; **Meyerbeer** Dinorah – *Ombre lègère qui suis mes pas (Shadow song) (Dinorah)*

Puccini Soprano Arias · MMO CDG 4053
Zvetelina Maldjanska–Plovdiv Philharmonic Orchestra/Todorov

La Bohème – *Mi chiamano Mimi (Mimi)*; La Bohème – *Quando men' vo' soletta la via (Musetta)*; La Bohème – *Donde lieta (Mimi)*; **Gianni Schicchi** – *O mio babbino caro (Lauretta)*; Turanodot – *Signore, ascolta! (Liu)*; Turandot – *Tu che di gel sei cinta (Liu)*

Soprano Arias · MMO CDG 4054
Ljudmila Gerova – Sofia Festival Orchestra/Todorov

W.A. Mozart Recitative and Aria – *Ergo Interest, an quìs...Quære Superna, KV. 143*; **Mozart** Le Nozze di Figaro – *Venite, inginocchiatevi (Susanna)*; **Mozart** Le Nozze di Figaro – *Giunse alfin il momento...Deh Vieni, non tardar (Susanna)*; **C.M. v.Weber** Der Freischütz – *Und ob die Wolke sie verhülle*; **Puccini** Tosca – *Vissi d'arte, vissi d'amore*

Donizetti Soprano Scenes & Arias · MMO CDG 4058
Zvetelina Maldjanska – Plovdiv Philharmonic/Todorov

Don Pasquale – Act I, Scene 4 *Quel guardo il cavaliere-So anch'io la virtú magica (Norina)*; Lucia di Lammermoor – Act I, Scene 2 *Quella fonte...– Regnava nel silenzio – Quando rapito in estasi (Lucia)*; Lucia di Lammermoor – Act II, Scene 5 *Il dolce suono – Ardon gl'Incensi – Alfin son tua – spargi d'amaro pianto (Lucia)*

Verdi Soprano Arias · MMO CDG 4059
Zvetelina Maldjanska – Plovdiv Philharmonic/Todorov

La Traviata – *è strano! è strano! (Violetta)*; I Vespri – *Siciliani (Siciliana d'Elena) Mercè, dilette amiche (Elena)*; Falstaff – *Sul fil d'un soffio etesio (Nannetta)*; Otello – *Piangea cantando (The Willow Song) (Desdemona)*; Rigoletto – *Caro nome (Gilda)*; La Traviata – Scene *Attendo, attendo...* and aria *Addio del passato (Violetta)*

Mozart Soprano Arias · MMO CDG 4060
Zvetelina Maldjanska – Plovdiv Philharmonic/Todorov

Die Entführung aus dem Serail – *Welcher Wechsel herrscht in meiner Seele...Traurigkeit ward mir zum Lose (Constanze)*; Die Entführung aus dem Serail – *Martern aller Arten (Constanze)*; Die Zauberflöte – *Ach, ich fühl's, es ist verschwunden (Pamina)*; Don Giovanni – *In quali eccessi, o Numi...Mi tradi quell' alma ingrata (Donna Elvira)*; Le Nozze di Figaro – *E Susanna non vien!...Dove sono I bei momenti (Contessa)*; Le Nozze di Figaro – *Giunse alfin il momento...Deh Vieni, non tardar (Susanna)*

Bellini Soprano Scenes & Arias · MMO CDG 4063
Zvetelina Maldjanska – Plovdiv Philharmonic/Todorov

Norma – *Casta diva...Fine al rito...Ah! bello a mi ritorna (Norma)*; I Puritani – *Qui la voce sua soave...Vien, diletto (Elvira)*

La Sonnambula: Soprano Scenes & Arias · MMO CDG 4064
Zvetelina Maldjanska – Plovdiv Philharmonic/Todorov

Care compagne...A te, diletta, tenera madre...Come per me sereno..Sovra il sen (Amina); Ah! Se una volta sola...Ah! non credea mirarti...Ah! Non giunge (Amina)

Mozart Soprano Arias Volume II · MMO CDG 4065
Snejana Dramtcheva - Plovdiv Philharmonic/Todorov

Die Zauberflöte O zitt're nicht, mein lieber Sohn...Zum Leiden bin ich auserkoren (Queen of the Night); Die Entführung aus dem Serail Durch Zärtlichkeit und Schmeicheln (Blonde); Die Entführung aus dem Serail Welche Wonne, welche Lust herrscht nun mehr in meiner Brust (Blonde); Così fan tutte Una donna a quindici anni (Despina); Don Giovanni Batti, batti, o bel Masetto (Zerlina); Don Giovanni Vedrai, carino, se sei buonino (Zerlina)

French Soprano Opera Arias · MMO CDG 4070
Upcoming Release–Complete titles available upon request.

MEZZO-SOPRANO

Verdi Mezzo-Soprano Arias · MMO CDG 4055
Ivanka Ninova–Sofia Festival Orchestra/Todorov

Il Trovatore – *Condotta ell'era in ceppi (Azucena)*; Il Trovatore – *Stride la vampa! (Azucena)*; Don Carlo – *O don fatale (Eboli)*; Don Carlo – *Nei giardin del bello (Eboli)*; Nabucco – *Oh, dischiuso, é il firmamento (Fenena)*

French & Italian Mezzo-Soprano Arias · MMO CDG 4062
Ivanka Ninova – Plovdiv Philharmonic/ Todorov

Mascagni Cavalleria Rusticana – *Voi lo sapete, o mama (Santuzza)*; **Ponchielli** La Gioconda – *Voce di donna o d'angelo (Cieca)*; **Saint-Saëns** Samson et Dalila – *Samson, recherchant ma présence (Dalila)*; **Bizet** Carmen – *L'amour est un oiseau rebelle (La Havanaise) (Carmen)*; **Donizetti** La Favorita– *Fia dunque vero? (Leonora)*; **Cilea** Adriana Lecouvreur – *Acerba volutta...Ogni eco, ogni ombra (La Principessa)*

Mozart Mezzo-Soprano Opera Arias · MMO CDG 4068
Upcoming Release–Complete titles available upon request.

John Wustman

In a field which is dominated by the vocal soloist, John Wustman is one of the few accompanists in this country who has achieved renown and critical acclaim in this most challenging of art forms. Mr. Wustman has developed that rare quality of bringing a strength and character to his accompaniments which create a true collaboration between the singer and the pianist. And this is as it should be, for in the art song especially, the piano part is not mere rhythmic and tonal background, but an integral part of the composer's intent and creation. Thus, on these records, Mr. Wustman provides not only the necessary accompaniment but also through his artistry, stylistic and interpretive suggestion for the study of the music.

Among the many artists he has accompanied in past years are: Gianna d'Angelo, Irina Arkhipova, Montserrat Caballe, Regine Crespin, Nicolai Gedda, Evelyn Lear, Mildred Miller, Anna Moffo, Birgit Nilsson, Jan Peerce, Roberta Peters, Elisabeth Schwarzkopf, Renata Scotto, Cesare Siepi, Giulietta Simionato, Thoms Stewart, Cesare Valetti and William Warfield.

Mr. Wustman has become known to millions of television viewers as the accompanist to Luciano Pavarotti in his many appearances in that medium.

BASS-BARITONE

Bass-Baritone Arias   MMO CDG 4056
Ivajlo Djourov – Sofia Festival Orchestra/Todorov

Mozart Le Nozze di Figaro – *Vertú mentr'io sospiro (Il Conte);* **Mozart** Le Nozze di Figaro – *Se vuol ballare, signor contino (Figaro);* **Rossini** Il Barbiere di Siviglia – *La callunia é un venticello (Basilio);* **Verdi** Simon Boccanegra – *Il lacerato spirito (Fiesco);* **Puccini** La Bohème – *Vecchia zimarra (Colline)*

Bass-Baritone Opera Arias Vol. II   MMO CDG 4066
Upcoming Release–Complete titles available upon request.

TENOR

Italian Tenor Arias   MMO CDG 4057
Kamen Tchanev – Plovdiv Philharmonic/Todorov

Puccini La Bohème – *Che gelida manina (Rodolfo);* **Puccini** Tosca – *Recondita armonia (Cavaradossi);* **Donizetti** L'Elisir d'Amore – *Una furtiva lagrima (Nemorino);* **Verdi** Rigoletto – *donna é mobile (Duca);* **Verdi** La Traviata scene and aria – *Lunge da Lei...De' miei bollenti spiriti (Alfredo)*

Puccini Tenor Arias   MMO CDG 4061
Vesselin Hristov–Plovdiv Philharmonic Orchestra/Todorov

Tosca – *Recondita armonia (Cavaradossi);* Tosca – *E lucevan le stelle (Cavaradossi);* Madama Butterfly – *Addio, Fiorito asil (Pinkerton);* Manon Lescaut – *Donna non vidi mai simile a questa (Des Grieux);* Turandot – *Non piangere, Liù! (Il Principe);* Turandot *Nessun dorma! (Calaf);* La Bohème – *Che gelida manina (Rodolfo)*

Verdi Tenor Opera Arias   MMO CDG 4067
Upcoming Release–Complete titles available upon request.

Tenor Arias from the Repertoire of Andrea Bocelli
Upcoming Release–Complete titles available upon request. MMO CDG 4069

HIGH VOICE

Schubert Lieder High Voice   MMO CD 4001

An Die Musik; Die Forelle; Auf Dem Wasser Zu Singen; Du Bist Die Ruh; Wohin?; Nach Und Taume; Standchen; Heidenroslein; Gretchen and Spinnrade; Der Musensohn; Romanze Aus "Rosamunde"; Lachen Und Weinen; Der Tod Und Das Madchen; An Silvia; Seligkeit

Schubert Lieder High Voice Vol. 2   MMO CD 4003

Fruhlingsglaube; Dass Sie Hier Gewesen; Im Fruhling; Die Liee Hat Gelogen; Du Liebst Mich Nicht; Erster Verlust; Die Allmacht; Ganymed; Wanderers Nachtlied; Nahe Des Geliebten; Fischerweise; Nachtviolen; Rastlose Liebe; Im Abendrot; Ungeduld

Brahms Lieder High Voice   MMO CD 4005

Liebestreu; Der Tod, Das Ist Die Kuhle Nacht; Wie Melodien Zieht Es Mir; Immer Leiser Wird Mein Schlummer; Stand-chen; Botschaft; O Wusst Ich Doch Den Weg Zuruck; Dein Blaues Auge; An Die Nachtigall; Bie Dir Sind Meine Gedanken; Von Ewiger Liebe; Die Mainacht; Sonntag; Vergebliches Standchen; Meine Liebe Ist Grun

Everybody's Favorite Songs High Voice   MMO CD 4007

Bach: My Heart Ever Faithful Gounod: Ave Maria Schubert: Ave Maria Brahms: Wiegenlied Franz: Dedication Dvorak: Songs My Mother Taught Me Tchaikovsky: None but the Lonely Heart Grieg: I Love Thee Hahn: Si Mes Vers Avaient Des Ailes Faure: Apres Un Reve Moore: Last Rose of Summer Johnson: Drink to Me Only with Thine Eyes Quilter: Now Sleeps the Crimson Petal Haydn: My Mother Bids Me Bind My Hair

Everybody's Favorite Songs High Voice Vol.2 MMO CD 4009

Purcell: Music for a While Torelli: Tu Lo Sai Mozart: Das Veilchen Handel: Where'er You Walk Beethoven: Ich Liebe Dich Schumann: Der Nussbaum, Die Lotasblume Schubert: Litanei Mendelssohn: On Wings of Song Bohm: Still Wie Die Nacht Traditional: Londonderry Air, Greensleeves Moore: Believe Me, If All Those Endearing Young Charms Debussy: Beau Soir Wolf: Verborgenheit Strauss: Zueignung

Laureate Series Recital Pieces

These editions feature recitals by established artists and accompaniments by fine pianists. Learn the songs by listening to the professional, then try them yourself. Selections are from the very best solo literature for the voice.

Beginning Soprano Solos
Kate Hurney/Bruce Eberle   **MMO CD 4041**

Bononcini: Per la gloria d'adorarvi **Haydn:** My Mother Bids Me Bind My Hair, **Old Melody:** WheLove Is Kind **Pergolesi:** Stizzoso, mio stizzoso **Purcell:** Man Is For the Woman Made **Sullivan:** The Moon And I **Weckerlin:** Bergere Legere and Jeune Fillette

Intermediate Soprano Solos
Kate Hurney/Bruce Eberle   **MMO CD 4042**

J.S. Bach: My Heart Ever Faithful **Brahms:** Vergebliches Standchen, **Duke:** Loveliest of Trees **Franck:** Panis Angelicus **Hahn:** Si mes vers avaient des aides **Mozart:** Das Veilchen **Paisiello:** Nel cor pin non mi sento **Puccini:** O Mio Babbino Caro

Beginning Mezzo Soprano Solos
Fay Kittelson/Richard Foster   **MMO CD 4043**

Barber: The Daisies **Beethoven:** Ich Liebe Dich **Campion:** Never Weather-Beaten Sail **Godard:** Chanson de Florian, **Hopkinson:** My Love is Gone to Sea **Niles:** I Wonder as I Wander **Pergolesi:** Se tu M'ami, Se Sospiri **Scarlatti:** O Cessate di Piagarmi **Schubert:** Haiden-Roslein **Thompson:** Velvet Shoes

Intermediate Mezzo Soprano Solos
Fay Kittelson/Richard Foster   **MMO CD 4044**

Brahms: Botschaft and der Tod, Das Ist die Kuhle Nacht **Handel:** Angels, Bright and Fair **Ives:** Children's Hour and a Night Song **Lotti:** Pur di Cesti, O Bocca Bella **Massenet:** Elegie **Persichetti:** The Microbe **Scarlatti:** Le Violette

Advanced Mezzo Soprano Solos
Fay Kittelson/Richard Foster   **MMO CD 4045**

Bach: Esurientes Implevit Bongs **Caccini:** Amarillo Mia Bella **Chausson:** Les Papillons **Faure:** Adieu and Apres un Reve **Guion:** At the Cry of the First Bird **Purcell:** When I Am Laid In Earth **Wolf:** Fussreise

Beginning Contralto Solos
Carline Ray/Bruce Eberle   **MMO CD 4046**

Brahms: Wiegenlied **Durante:** Vergin, Tutto Amor **Franz:** Es Had die Rose Sichbeklagt **MacGimsey:** Sweet Little Jesus Boy **Monteverdi:** Lasciatemi morire! **Mozart:** Die Ante **Scarlatti:** Se Florindo e Fedele **Spiritual:** Ride On, King Jesus!

Beginning Tenor Solos
George Shirley/Wayne Sanders   **MMO CD 4047**

Handel: Ombra Mat Fu **McGill:** Duna **Purcell:** If Music Be the Food of Love **Scarlatti:** Cara, Cara e Dolce **Schubert:** Das Wandern **Shirley (arr.):** There is a Balm in Gilead

Intermediate Tenor Solos
George Shirley/Wayne Sanders   **MMO CD 4048**

Dello Joio: There is a Lady Sweet and Kind **Leoncavallo:** Mattinata **Massenet:** Crepuscule **Mendelssohn:** Be Thou Faithful (Elijah) **Rachmaninoff:** In the Silence of Night **Swanson:** Night Song

Advanced Tenor Solos
George Shirley/Wayne Sanders   **MMO CD 4049**

Faure: Fleur Jette **Handel:** Every Valley (Messiah) **Scarlatti:** Sono Unite a Tormentarmi **Schubert:** Die Allmacht **Swanson:** Joy **Verdi:** Questra o Quella (Rigoletto)

Music Minus One . • 50 Executive Boulevard • Elmsford, New York 10523-1325
http://www.musicminusone.com   914-592-1188 • fax 914-592-3575 • mmomus@aol.com   http://www.pocketsongs.com

17th/18th Century Italian Songs
High Voice   MMO CD 4011

Caldara: Selve Amiche **Carissimi:** Vittoria, Mio Cuore **Monteverdi:** Lasciatemi Morire **Scarlatti:** Gia Il Sole Dal Gange **Caccini:** Udite, Amanti, Belle Rose Purpurine, Sfogava Conle Stelle **Cavalli:** Sospiri di Fuoco **Falconieri:** Bella Porta Di Rubini **Durante** Vergin, Tutto Amor **Giordani:** Caro Mio Ben **Peri:** Nel Puro Ardor **Scarlatti:** Sento Nel Core

17th/18th Century Italian Songs
High Voice Vol.2   MMO CD 4013

Caccini: Amarilli **Legrenzi:** Che Fiero Costume **Durante:** Danza, Danza Fanciulla **Caccini:** Occhi Immortali **Cavalli:** Son Ancor Pargoletta **Scarlatti:** O Cessate di Piagarmi, Toglietemi La Vita Ancor **Staradella:** Se Nel Ben Sempre **Falconieri:** Occhietti Amati **Rontani:** Caldi Sospiri **Monteverdi:** Illustratevi, O Cieli **Rosa:** Vado Ben Spesso Cangiando Loco **Peri:** Gioite al Canto Mio

Hugo Wolf Lieder High Voice   MMO CD 4020

Im Fruhling; Auf Ein Altes Bild; Gebet; Lebe Wohl; In Der Fruhe; Begegnung; Der Gartner; Schlafendes Jesuskind; Nun Lass Uns Frieden Schliessen; Verschwiegene Liebe; Nachtzauber; Herr, Was Tragt Der Boden Hier; Ach, Des Knaben Augen; Anakreons Grab; Epiphanias

Richard Strauss Lieder High Voice   MMO CD 4022

Heimliche Afforderung; Allerseelen; Heimkehr; Nacht; Morgen; Wie Sollten Wir Geheim; Wiegenlied; Befreit; Waldseligkeit; Freundliche Vision; Mein Auge; Traum Durch Die Dammerung; Standchen; Ich Schwebe; Cacilie

Robert Schumann Lieder High Voice   MMO CD 4024

Ruckert - Widmung; Heine - Du Bist Wie Eine Blume; Eichendorff - In De Fremde; Eichendorff - Waldesgesprach, Mondnacht, Fruhlingsnach; Ruckert - Der Himmel Hat Eine Trane Geweint; Heine - Dein Angesicht; Kerner - Stille Tranen; Heine - Ich Grolle Nicht; Altkatholisches Gedicht - Requiem; Lenau - Meine Rose; Heine - Mit Myrten Und Rosen; Ruckert - Mein Schoner Stern; Heine - Schone Wiege Meiner Leiden

17th/18th Century Italian Songs
Low Voice   MMO CD 4012

Caldara: Selve Amiche **Carissimi:** Vittoria, Mio Cuore **Monteverdi:** Lasciatemi Morire **Scarlatti:** Gia Il Sole Dal Gange **Caccini:** Udite, Amanti, Belle Rose Purpurine, Sfogava Conle Stelle **Cavalli:** Sospiri di Fuoco **Falconieri:** Bella Porta di Rubini **Durante:** Vergin, Tutto Amor **Giordani:** Caro Mio Ben **Peri:** Nel Puro Ardor **Scarlatti:** Sento Nel Core

17th/18th Century Italian Songs
Low Voice Vol. 2   MMO CD 4014

Caccini: Amarilli **Legrenzi:** Che Fiero Costume **Durante:** Danza, Danza Fanciulla **Caccini:** Occhi Immortali **Cavalli:** Son Ancor Pargoletta **Scarlatti:** O Cessate di Piagarmi, Toglietemi La Vita Ancor **Staradella:** Se Nel Ben Sempre; **Falconieri:** Occhietti Amati; **Rontani:** Caldi Sospiri **Monteverdi:** Illustratevi, O Cieli **Rosa:** Vado Ben Spesso Cangiando Loco **Peri:** Gioite Al Canto Mio

Hugo Wolf Lieder Low Voice   MMO CD 4021

Im Fruhling; Auf Ein Altes Bild; Gebet; Lebe Wohl; In Der Fruhe; Auf Einer Wanderung; Der Gartner; Schlafendes Jesuskind; Um Mitternacht; Verschwiegene Liebe; Nachtzauber; Herr, Was Tragt Der Boden Hier; Ach, Des Knaben Augen; Nun Lass Uns Frieden Schliessen; Anakreons Grab

Richard Strauss Low Voice   MMO CD 4023

Heimliche Afforderung; Allerseelen; Heimkehr; Die Nacht; Morgen; Wie Sollten Wir Geheim; Du Meines Herzens Krohelen; Befreit; Waldseligkeit; Freundliche Vision; Ich Trage Meine Minne; Traum Durch Die Dammerung; Standchen; Ich Schwebe; Cacilie

Robert Schumann Lieder Low Voice   MMO CD 4025

Ruckert - Widmung; Heine - Du Bist Wie Eine Blume; Eichendorff - In De Fremde, Waldesgesprach, Mondnacht, Fruhlingsnach; Ruckert - Der Himmel Hat Eine Trane Geweint; Heine - Dein Angesicht; Kerner - Stille Tranen; Heine - Ich Grolle Nicht; Byron - Aus Den Hebraischen Gesangen; Lenau - Meine Rose; Heine - Mit Myrten Und Rosen; Ruckert - Mein Schoner Stern!; Heine - Schone Wiege Meiner Leide

---

LOW VOICE

Schubert Lieder Low Voice   MMO CD 4002

An Die Musik; Auf Dem Wasser Zu Singen; Du Bist Die Ruh; Wohin?; Nach Und Taume; Standchen; Heidenroslein; Gretchen and Spinnrade; Der Musensohn; Romanze Aus "Rosamunde"; Der Tod Und Das Madchen; An Silvia; Seligkeit; Erikonig

Schubert Lieder Low Voice Vol. 2   MMO CD 4004

Fruhlingsglaube; Dass Sie Hier Gewesen; Im Fruhling; Die Liee Hat Gelogen; Du Liebst Mich Nicht; Erster Verlust; Die Allmacht; Ganymed; Wanderers Nachtlied/; Nahe Des Geliebten; Fischerweise; Nachtviolen; Rastlose Liebe; Im Abendrot; Ungeduld

Brahms Lieder Low Voice   MMO CD 4006

Liebestreu; Sapphische Ode; Wie Melodien Zieht Es Mir; Im-mer Leiser Wird Mein Schlummer; Standchen; Botschaft; O Wusst Ich Doch Den Weg Zuruck; Dein Blaues Auge; An Die Nachtigall; Von Ewiger Liebe; Die Mainacht; Sonntag; Verge-bliches Standchen; Meine Liebe Ist Grun; Auf dem Kirchofe

Everybody's Favorite Songs Low Voice   MMO CD 4008

Bach: My Heart Ever Faithful **Gounod:** Ave Maria **Schubert:** Ave Maria **Brahms:** Wiegenlied **Franz:** Dedication **Dvorak:** Songs My Mother Taught Me **Tchaikovsky:** None But the Lonely Heart **Grieg:** I Love Thee **Hahn:** Si Mes Vers Avaient Des Ailes **Faure:** Apres Un Reve **Moore:** Last Rose of Summer **Johnson:** Drink to Me Only With Thine Eyes **Quilter:** Now Sleeps the Crimson Petal **Haydn:** My Mother Bids Me Bind My Hair

Everybody's Favorite Songs
Low Voice Vol. 2   MMO CD 4010

Purcell: Music for a While **Torelli:** Tu Lo Sai **Mozart:** Das Veilchen **Handel:** Where'er You Walk **Beethoven:** Ich Liebe Dich **Schumann:** Der Nussbaum, Die Lotasblume **Schubert:** Litanei **Mendelssohn:** On Wings of Song **Bohm:** Still Wie Die Nacht **Traditional:** Londonderry Air, Greensleeves **Moore:** Believe Me, If All Those Endearing Young Charms **Debussy:** Beau Soir **Wolf:** Verborgenheit **Strauss:** Zueignung

---

Opera Releases are $34.98 each.
Wustman & Laureate Albums are $29.98 each.
2 CD sets are $39.98 each.

SOPRANO

Famous Soprano Arias · MMO CDG 4015
Mozart: The Magic Flute -Ach, Ich Fuhl's; The Marriage of Figaro -Deh Vieni, Non Tardar **Puccini:** La Boheme - Mi Chiamano Mimi, Quando M'en Vo; Madama Butterfly - Un Bel Di Vedremo; La Traviata - Addio, Del Passato; Otello -Ave Maria **Verdi:** Falstaff - Sul Fil D'un Soffio Etesio **Weber:** Freischutz - Und Ob Die Wolke **Puccini:** Gianni Schicchi - O Mio Babbino Caro **Charpentier:** Louise -Depuis le Jour **Massenet:** Manon - Adieu, Notre Petite Table **Gounod:** Faust - Jewel Song

Mozart Arias Soprano · MMO CD 4026
Cosi Fan Tutte - Come Scoglio; Don Giovanni - Non Mi Dir; Le Nozze di Figaro - Porgi, Amor, Qualche Ris, Dove Sono; Cosi Fan Tutte' - In Vomini, Una Donna A Quindici Anni; Don Giovanni - Batti,Batti, O Bel Masetto; Verdrai, Carino , Se Sei Buono; The Abduction from the Seraglio-Ach,Ich Liebt

Verdi Arias Soprano · MMO CD 4027
La Forza Del Destino - Pace,Pace,Mio Dio; Ernani -Ernani, In Volami; Un Ballo in Maschera - Morro, Mi Prima In Graz; Il Trovatore' - D'amor Sull' Ali Rosee; Don Carlo -Tu Che Le Vanita; Aida - Oh Patria Mie; Macbeth - Sleepwalking Scene - Una Maccia

Italian Arias Soprano · MMO CD 4028
Handel: Julius Caesar - Vadoro Pupille, Piangero **Rossini:** William Tell -Selva Opaca **Puccini:** La Boheme - Donde Lieta Usci **Mascagni:** Cavalleria Rusticana -Voi Lo Sapete; Cilea: Adriana Lecouvreur -Io Son L'umile Ancella, Poveri Fiori **Catalani:** La Wally - Ebben, N'andro Lontana; Boito: Mefistofele - L'altra Notte **Ponchielli:** La Gioconda - Suicidio

French Arias Soprano · MMO CD 4029
Gluck: Alceste - Divinites Du Styx; Iphigenie En Tauride - O Malheureuse Iphigeni **Massenet:** Le Cid - Pleurez! Pleurez, Mes Yeux! **Debussy:** L'enfant Prodigue - Recitative and Lia's Aria; Bizet: Carmen - Je Dis Que Rien Ne M'epouvante **Massenet:** Herodiade - Il est Doux, Il Est Bon **Gounod:** Faust - The King of Thule; Sapho - O Ma Lyre Immortelle

MEZZO-SOPRANO

Famous Mezzo-Soprano Arias · MMO CDG 4016
Gluck: Orfeo - Che Faro Senza Euridice **Handel:** Xerxes -Largo **Mozart:** Marriage of Figaro -Voi Che Sapete, Non So Piu Cosa Son **Thomas:** Mignon - Connais Tu Le Pays? **Ponchielli:** La Gioconda -Voce di Donna **Verdi:** Il Trovatore -Stride La Vampa **Saint-Saens:** Samson et Dalila - Printemps Qui Commence, Amour, Viens Aider; Mon Coeur S'ouvre A Ta Vo **Bizet:** Carmen - Habanera, Seguidilla

When thinking about **Music Minus One**, there is no finer present you can send a loved one; nothing more unique or longer lasting in the pleasure it provides then an opera, orchestra or chamber ensemble.
Detach below and send to Music Minus One
50 Executive Blvd. Elmsford, NY 10523-1325,
FAX 914-592-3116 or call toll-free 800-669-7464

TENOR

Famous Tenor Arias · MMO CDG 4017
Mozart: The Magic Flute - Dies Bildnis; Don Giovanni - Dalla Sua Pace **Verdi:** La Traviata - De' Miei Bollenti Spiriti; Rigoletto - La Donna E Mobile; Lalo: Le Roi D'ys - Aubade **Gounod:** Faust - Salut! Demeure Chaste et Pure **Massenet:** Manon - Le Reve **Flotow:** Martha - M'appari; **Giordano:** Fedora - Amor Ti Vieta **Puccini:** Manon Lescaut - Donna Non Vidi Mai; Tosca - E Lucevan Le Stelle; La Boheme - Che Gelida Manina **Bizet:** Carmen - Flower Song

BARITONE

Famous Baritone Arias · MMO CDG 4018
Mozart: The Marriage of Figaro - Non Piu Andrai; Don Giovanni - Deh Vieni Alla Finestra; The Magic Flute - Der Vogelfanger Bin Ich Ja **Gounod:** Faust - Avant de Quitter Ces Lieux (Eb)(Db); **Verdi:** Il Trovatore -Il Balen Del Suo Soriso; La Traviato - Di Provenza Il Mar; Un Ballo In Maschera - Alla Vita Che T'arride, Eir Tu Che Macchiavi **Bizet:** Carmen - Toreador Song **Leoncavallo:** I Pagliacci - Prologue **Massenet:** Herodiade - Vision Fugitive **Wagner:** Tannhauser - O Du Mein Holder Abendstern

BASS

Famous Bass Arias · MMO CDG 4019
Mozart: The Magic Flute - O Isis Und Osiris, In Diesen Heil'gen Hallen; The Marriage of Figaro - Non Piu Andrai;**Gounod:** Faust - Vous Qui Faites L'endormie (Serenade), Le Veau D'or **Puccini:** La Boheme - Vecchia Zimmara **Verdi:** Falstaff - Quand'ero Paggio **Rossini:** The Barber of Seville - La Calunnia **Bellini:** La Sonnambula - Vi Ravviso, O Luoghi Ameni **Verdi:** Ernani - Infelice! E Tuo Cedevi; Don Carlo - Ella Giammai Mamo; Simone Boccanegra - Il Lacerto Spirito

ORATORIO ARIAS

Soprano Oratorio Arias · MMO CD 4030
Mozart: Alleluia, Et Incarnatus Est **Haydn:** On Mighty Wings, With Verdure Clad **Mendelssohn:** Hear Ye Israel! **Bach:** Ich Will Dir Mein Herze Schenken, Blute Nur **Handel:** Rejoice, Rejoice Greatly, Come Unto Him, I Know That My Redeemer Liveth

Alto Oratorio Arias · MMO CD 4031
Handel: O Thou That Tellest Good Tidings To Zion, He Shall Feed His Flock, Thou Shall Bring Them In, In The Battle **Bach:** Prepare Thyself, Zion, Keep, O My Spirit, Buss' Und Reu', Erbarme Dich **Mendelssohn:** Prepare Thyself, ZionBut the Lord is Mindful; O Rest In The Lord

Tenor Oratorio Arias · MMO CD 4032
Handel: Comfort Ye, Every Valley, Thou Shall Break Them, Waft Her, Angels; In Native Worth; Sound An Alarm! **Bach:** Deposuit **Mendelssohn:** If With All Your Hearts **Mendelssohn:** Then Shall The Righteous **Verdi:** Ingemisco

Bass Oratorio Arias · MMO CD 4033
Haydn: Now Shines The Greatest Glory Of Heaven **Handel:** But Who May Abide The Day Of His Coming, The Trumpet Shall Sound, Why Do The Nations, Honor And Arms, Arm, Arm, Ye Brave! **Mendelssohn:** Lord God Of Abraham, Is Not His Word Like Fire?, It Is Enough **Verdi:** Confutatis

---

Send to:

NAME

ADDRESS

CITY   STATE   ZIP

PHONE   FAX   EMAIL

Bill to:

NAME

ADDRESS

CITY   STATE   ZIP

PHONE   FAX   EMAIL

Please charge my:

☐ MasterCard   ☐ VISA   ☐ DISCOVER   ☐ American Express

CARD NO: EXP DATE:

SIGNATURE

Items not released will be maintained on back order.
You will not be charged for items until shipment is made.

All Opera Releases are $34.98 each.
All Wustman & Laureate Albums are $29.98 each.
2 CD sets are $39.98 each.

Items: MMO#_____   MMO#_____   MMO#_____   MMO#_____

MMO#_____   MMO#_____   MMO#_____   MMO#_____